★ ★ ★ ★ ★

Palate
Palette

Tasty Illustrations from
Around the World

20th Anniviction:ary

Palate Palette

Tasty Illustrations from Around the World

First published and distributed by
viction:workshop ltd.

viction:ary™

viction:workshop ltd.
Unit C, 7/F, Seabright Plaza,
9-23 Shell Street,
North Point, Hong Kong
Url: victionary.com
Email: we@victionary.com

🅕 @victionworkshop
🅞 @victionworkshop
Bē @victionary
🅟 @victionary

Edited and produced by viction:ary
Creative direction by Victor Cheung
Book design by viction:workshop ltd.
Cover illustrations by Anke Knapper, DON MAK
& CO., Family Meal, Hiroyuki Yamada, Mao
Hagiwara, Victoria Moey and Xiha
©2021 viction:workshop ltd.

ISBN 978-988-74628-0-4
Printed and bound in China

DELIGHTFUL CUISINE

DRAWN FROM SCRATCH

Preface

BY VICTIONARY

What is there to say about food that has
not already been said?

Figuratively speaking, whether you eat to live or live to eat, food
is the fuel that makes the world go 'round! Besides its obvious
purpose as a means of sustenance that ensures the survival
of all living creatures on this planet, it also serves as so much
more for many – an adhesive that binds generations of a family
together; a conversation starter with a stranger; or a blank
canvas for expressing one's raw passion or talent.

Cooking teacher, author, and television personality Julia Child,
who is credited for bringing French cuisine to the American
public, once famously stated that 'people who love to eat are
always the best people' and it is hard to disagree, due to a
joie de vivre that they always seem to be filled with. In fact,
this sentiment extends to those who take pleasure in cooking
for others. Food can be inspiring, comforting, and nourishing
in a single bite, even when prepared with the humblest of
ingredients, and are alchemies of joy that often taste better
when shared. As such, it comes as no surprise that the simple
act of making and/or enjoying a meal with company has been
proven to boost happiness all around.

In many parts of Asia, food is still a wordless way to show care or concern; morsels of history seared in memory; and an inextricable part of one's background or identity. Due to how big and diverse the continent is (~44.58 million km²!), flavour profiles can vary greatly even between neighbouring states, but it makes for one gigantic melting pot of cultures that would excite any foodie looking for a gastronomic adventure. With more modern influences being mixed into traditional rituals and a growing number of East-meets-West recipes for F&B success, it is interesting to see what the future holds.

As a publisher based in Hong Kong, we are extremely lucky to be exposed to a delicious culinary mishmash – a fact that inspired us to highlight the amazing artists and illustrators who feature food (and its many drool-worthy facets) as the main theme in their work. The research that we did for one of our 2019 releases, 'BRANDLife: Restaurants & Bars'—where we showcased some of the best eateries and bars today that know how important it is to not only consider the quality of food being offered, but also the visual identities and interiors that have the power to shape diners' experiences in catering to our multi-sensorial nature as human-beings—also had a hand in shaping the direction of this book.

While 'BRANDLife' taught us that it takes a lot to bring a menu to life in a commercially viable manner, 'Palate Palette' goes the opposite way by celebrating the purity of the creative idea through beautiful expressions of shapes, colours, lines, and textures that you can almost taste. We hope that you will savour the yummy drawings and charming handwritten notes on these pages as much as we do!

Bon Appétit

Hiroyuki Yamada

HATABO Store Poster: [L] Hakusai [R] Kabu
Client: Japan-Korea Creative Restaurant HATABO

HATABO Store Poster: [L] Maitake [R] Simeji/Shiitake
Client: Japan-Korea Creative Restaurant HATABO

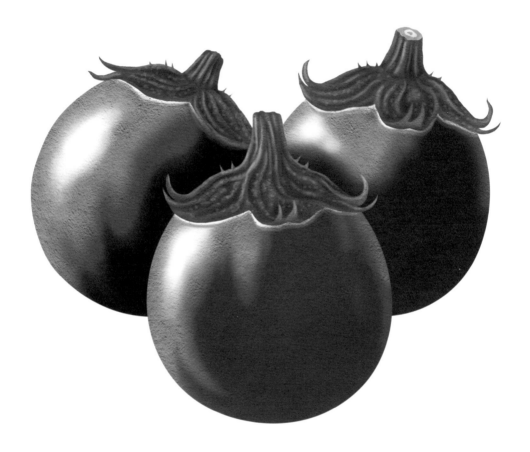

Japan Agricultural Cooperatives PR Magazine: [L] Tomato [R] Kamo Nasu
Client: Japan Agricultural Cooperatives

Everyone praised me, "It looks delicious!!"
I'm asked to do a lot of work to draw food.

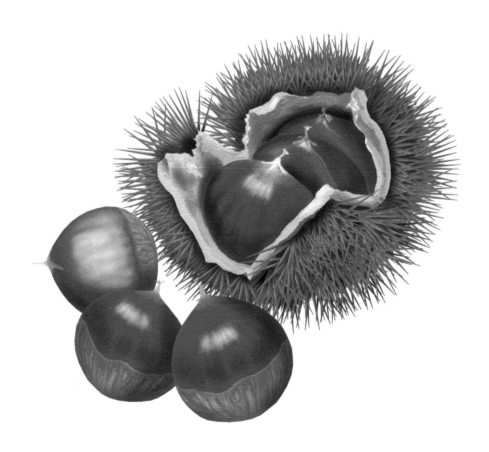

Japan Agricultural Cooperatives PR Magazine: [L] Tanbakuri [R] Meron
Client: Japan Agricultural Cooperatives

[L][R] Frozen Bread Packaging Illustrations
Client: STYLE BREAD

Yuko Kurihara

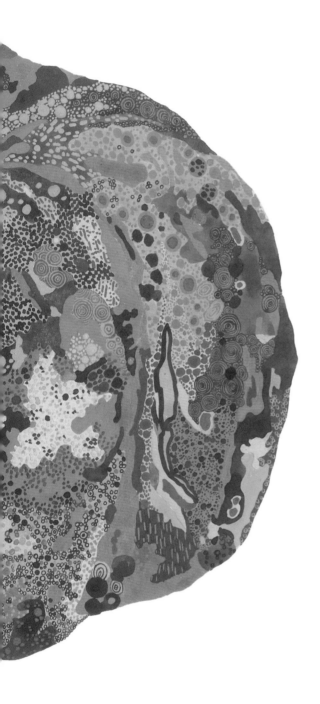

Pumpkin

Yuko Kurihara

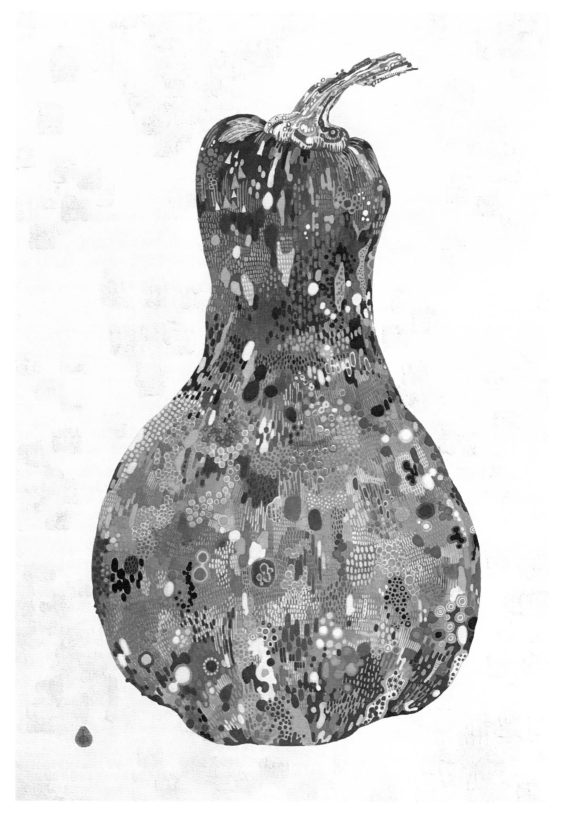

[L] Pione [R] Jadepumpkin

The color and texture of meat and fish

Why do I like to draw food?

Stregth and interesting patterns of Vegetables

Fruits have a lovely form and color

Every ingredient has an attractive point, so I never get tired of drawing them.

YUKO 栗原由子
KURIHARA

Yuko Kurihara

[R] Red Beets Gold Beets

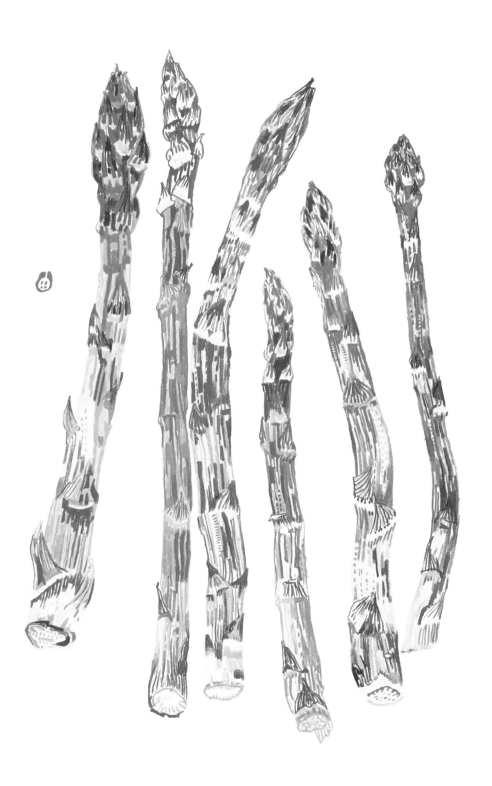

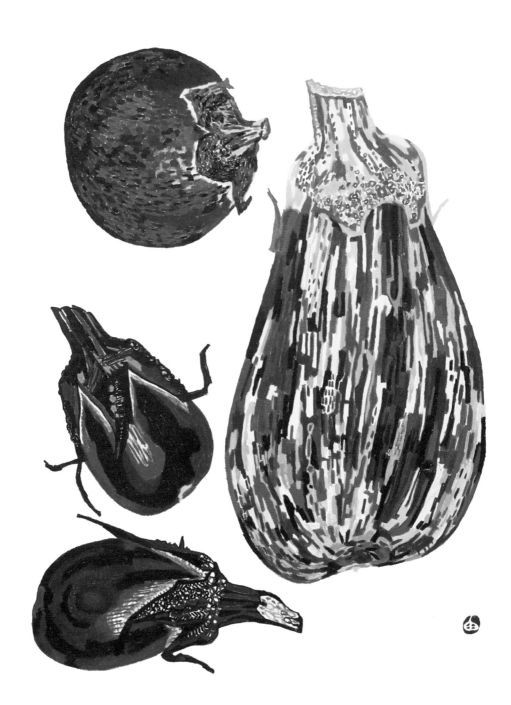

[L] Asparagus [R] Eggplant

Claire Harrup

[L] Waitrose Home Rebranding: Eggs [R] The Bountiful Kitchen
Client: [L] Waitrose [R] Kyle Books

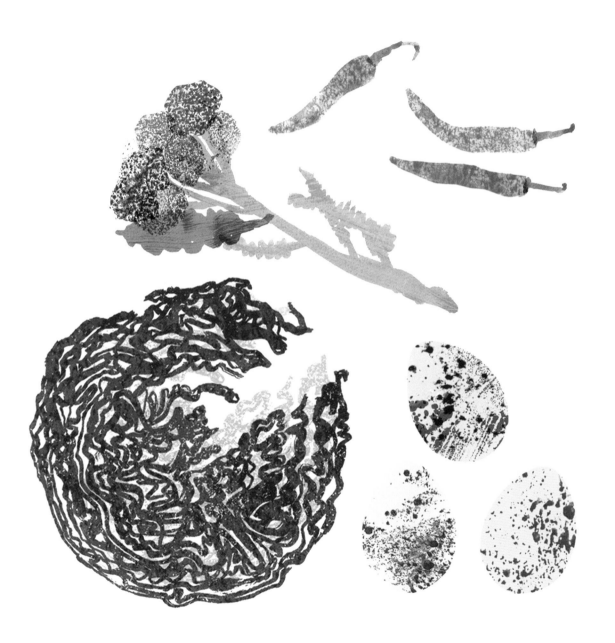

Claire Harrup

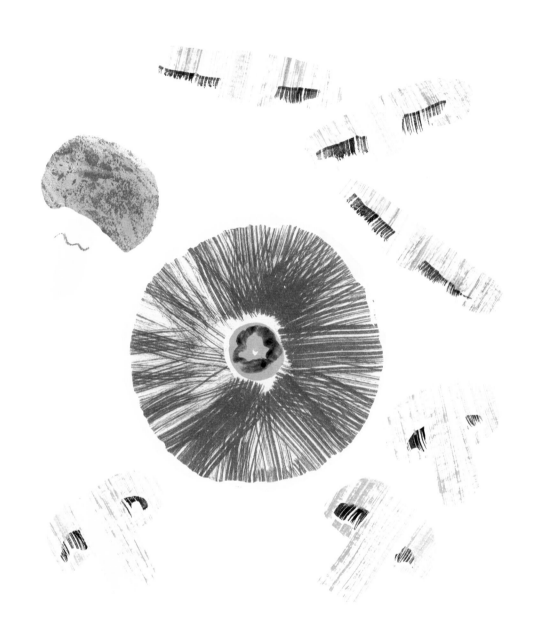

[L] The Bountiful Kitchen [R] Waitrose Home Rebranding: Mushrooms
Client: [L] Kyle Books [R] Waitrose

I enjoy drawing food because it allows me to play with a variety of colours, textures and organic shapes, finding playful ways of representing the familiar.

Luckily my husband is an excellent cook! My favourite are his homemade pizzas, eaten in our kitchen with our children.

[L] Waitrose Home Rebranding: Leeks
Client: Waitrose

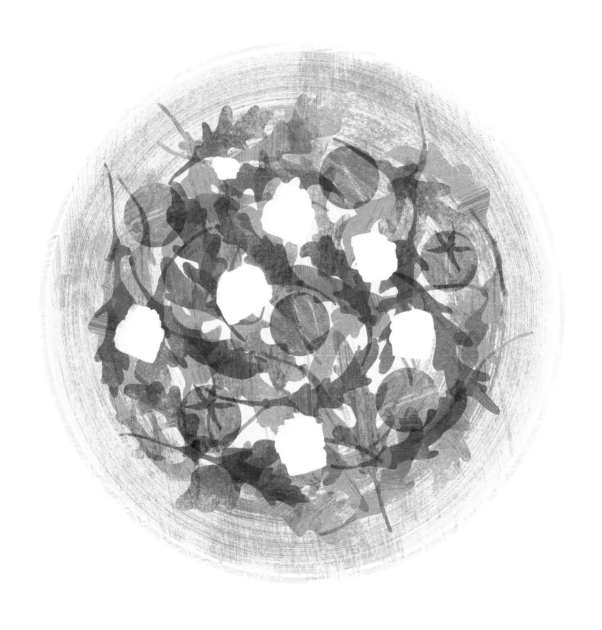

Waitrose Home Rebranding: [L] Salad Bowl [R] Pizza
Client: Waitrose

Hatsue Fujiyasu

[L] Spangle Tea of Fomalhaut　[R] Mayer Lemon Tart

[L] Soup [R] Breakfast

I feel some stories in the foods.
When I draw food, I want to draw the warm
and happy atmosphere that food exudes.

[L] Picnic [R] Waterside

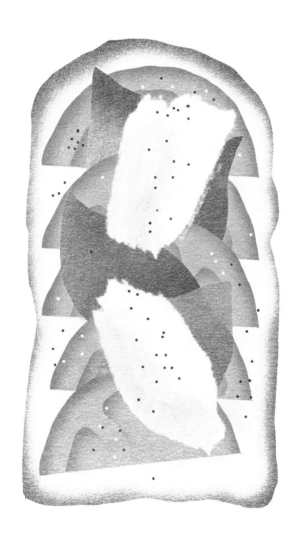

Keiji Yano

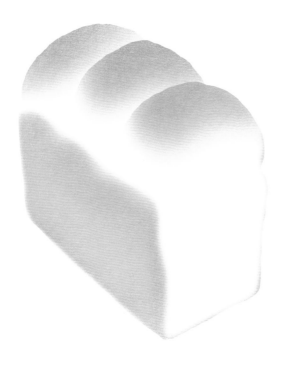

[L][R] Bread Illustrations
Special Credit: OFFICE YANO inc.

In human desire, the appetite is big.

I drool when I see delicious food.

They believe that delicious-looking food
visually ruvigorates people.

Keiji Yano

[L][R] Food Illustrations
Special Credit: OFFICE YANO inc.

Midori Asano

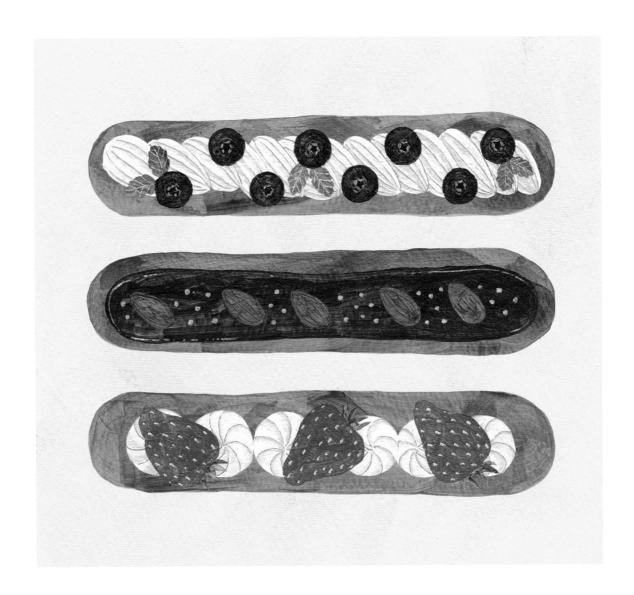

Apple

Grape

Pear

[L] Apples for 3 o'clock [R] Autumn Fruits

Midori Asano

Because it makes me happy.

Ayu Iwashima

Savi no Niwa Postcard
Client: Savi no Niwa

coffee cup diarys

コーヒーカップ ダイアリーズ

[L] Coffee Cup Diaries [R] Meat Preparation /
Grilled Baby Carrots / Lemonade
[L] Client: Weekend Books

ほしや

[L] Hoshiya Postcard [R] Minestrone Soup
Client: [L] Hoshiya [R] Kodansha

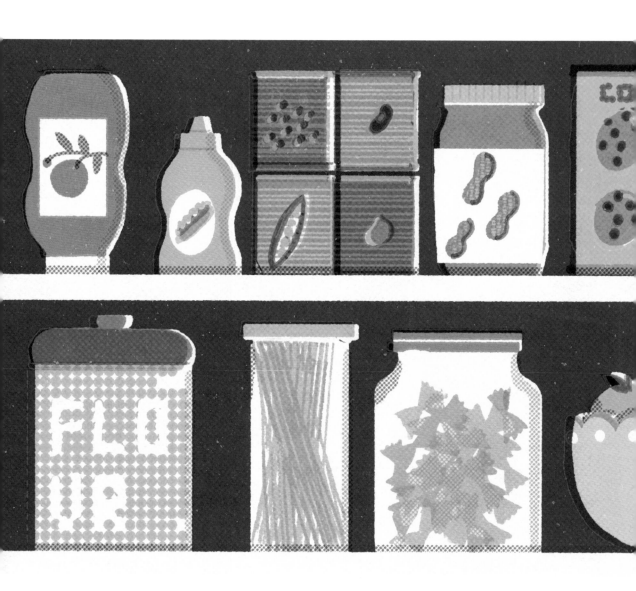

Lucia Calfapietra

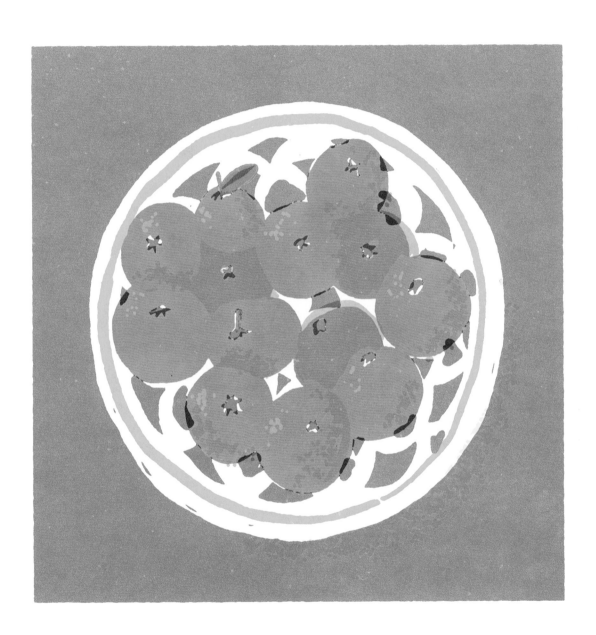

[L] Cherry Pie [R] Clementines

[L] Breakfast [R] Candies
[R] Client: Bienmanger.com

Jordan Amy Lee

[L] Left My Bag at Home [R] Ragu with Tagliatelle

Jordan Amy Lee

[L] Still Life of Picnic [R] Still Life with Cake and Flowers

Food is what inspires me to make art the most.
The shapes colours and textures of different fruits
and vegetables, and pretty much any other food,
are so intrinsically beautiful and unique, I find it hard
not to visualise a piece of art when I look at them;
picturing different compositions and possibilities for new
illustrations in my head.

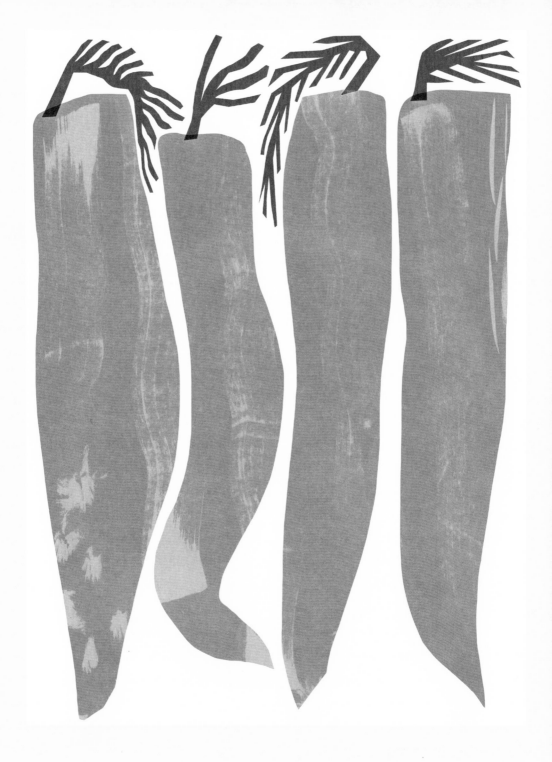

[L] Mushrooms [R] Carrots

Xiha

[L] Shakshuka [R] Omurice
[L] Client: MONOCLE

[L] Bibimbab [R] Full English Breakfast

Like I am happy when I eat delicious food
I feel happy when I draw a delicious illustration.
I also enjoy imagining the taste.
I want other people to be happy
after seeing my illustration.

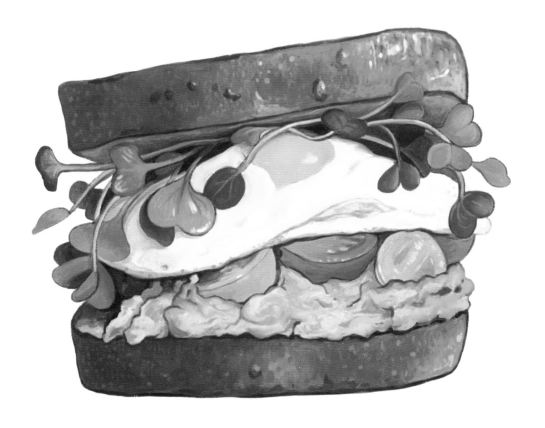

|L| Triple Cheese Burger |R| Avocado Sandwich

[L] Donuts [R] Fluffy Pancakes
[R] Client: MONOCLE

Victoria Moey

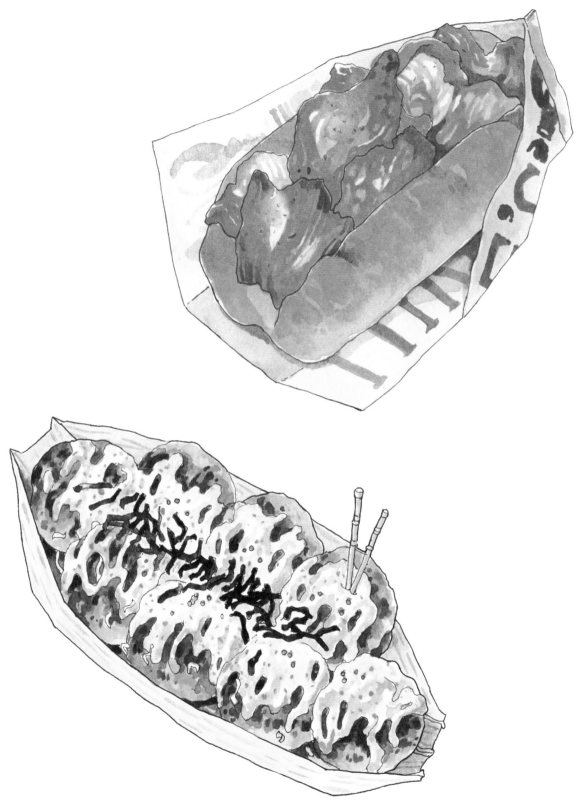

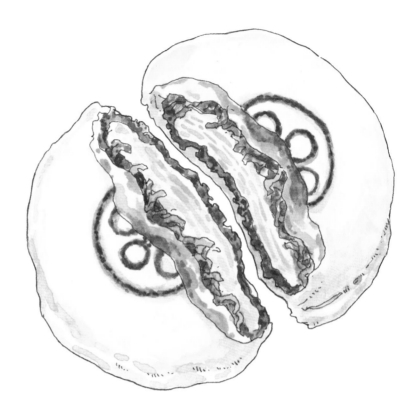

Japan Trip Food Journal: |L| Lobster Roll / Takoyaki
|R| Tonkatsu / Sweet Potato

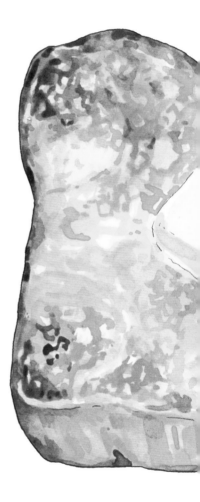

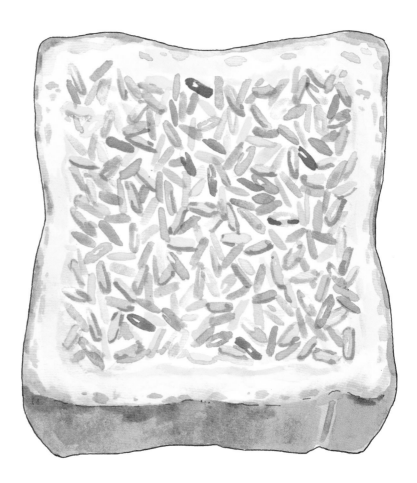

[L][R] Bread & Butter: Strawberry Banana Toast / French Toast / Fairy Toast

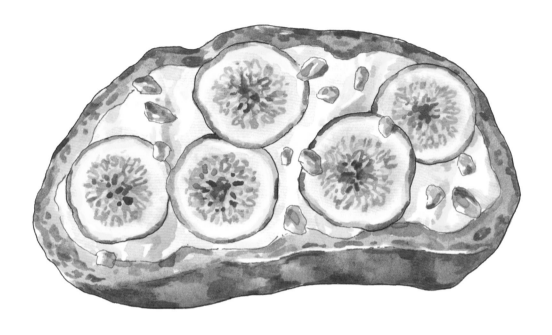

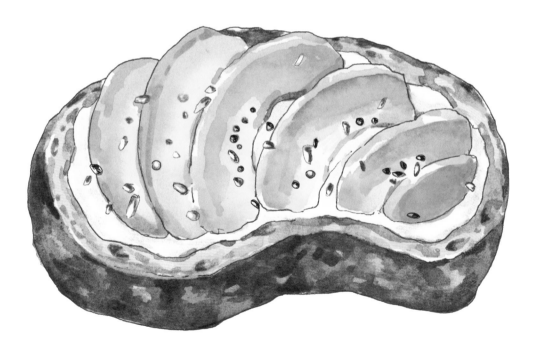

[L] Japan Trip Food Journal: Grape Cake / Crepe / Donut Ring
[R] Bread & Butter: Fig Toast / Avocado Toast

Claire Chien

[L||R] Traditional Festival in Asia - Mid-Autumn Festival, Traditional Food Illustration

Claire Chien

I enjoy drinking wine, and delicate wine
requires delicate food. So I always pay
special attention to pictures of food.

Because of this, I became obsessed
with attractive food. I always
want to draw it with my own
paintbrush when I see one.

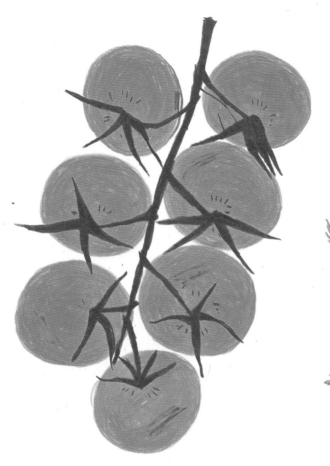

Xuetong Wang

食べる: [L] Tomatoes / Carrot [R] Summer Radish / Pumpkin

食べる: [L] Soup Curry / Ramen [R] Sashimidon / Tonkatsu

I like to draw food because the diversity of foods makes me so interested in it. So many different colors, shapes, flavors, and stories. More important, food makes people happy, and I really enjoy exploring the cultures and stories related to different food.

食べる： [L] Yakitori / Fruit Tea / Wonton [R] Souffle

DONMAK & CO.

[L||R] Vintage Mooncake Shops in Hong Kong
Client: Apple Daily HK | Project Assistant: Esther Man

[L] Ramen [R] Wonton Noodle
Client: Apple Daily HK

[L][R] Food Illustrations
Client: Apple Daily HK

[L][R] Menu Illustrations
Client: Nespresso Boutique IFC | Agency: Destination Design & Production

Harapekomegane

[L] Sukiyaki Harapekojirushi2 [R] Hennaoden
Client: [L] Nijinoehonya [R] Graphic-sha Publishing Co., Ltd

どかっと　おおきな　かたまりにく。

あふれでる　にくじゅうで　つくった　グレービーソースを
たらりと　かけて　くちに　いれたら
こりゃ　たまらぬ。

どうじゃ、これが
にくのなかの　にく。

ローストビーフを　あいする
われこそが、
にくのくに　いちばんの
王さま　である。

うまい　うまい！
ひとくちだって
やるものか！

NikunoKuni
Client: KYOUIKUGAGEKI.Co

みんなのおすし

はらぺこめがね

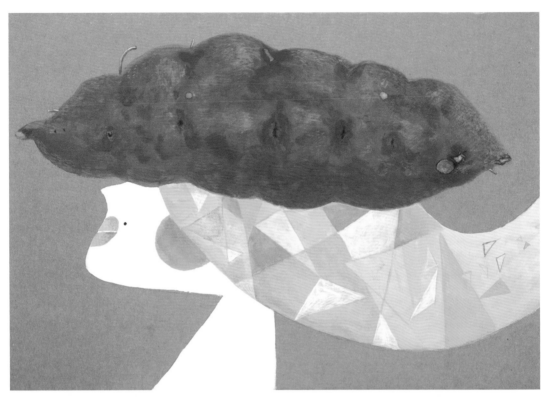

[L] MinnanoOsushi [R] Sweet Potato Girl / Strawberry Girl
[L] Client: POPLAR Publishing Co., Ltd.

Family Meal

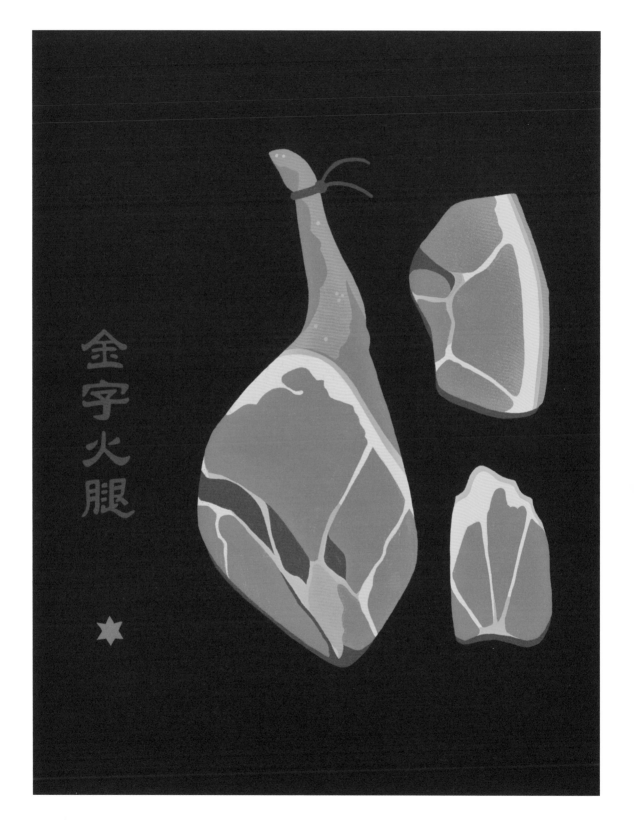

金字火腿

[L] Salmon [R] Jinhua Ham

[L] Japan [R] Milk & Coffee Swirl
[L] Client: Compound Butter Magazine | Art Direction: Jaya Nicely

I LOVE EXPLORING THE JOY AND EXCITEMENT
WE FEEL WHEN WE SEE IMAGES OF FOOD.
IT CAN BE FUELED BY A CRAVING FOR
OUR FAVORITE MEAL, NOSTALGIA FOR A
CHILDHOOD SNACK, OR THE THE PLEASANT
SHAPE OF A WELL-BAKED PASTRY.

I WANT TO MAKE PEOPLE SMILE THROUGH
THOUGHTFUL ILLUSTRATIONS OF FOOD! :)

[L] Korean Fried Chicken & Beer [R] Potstickers

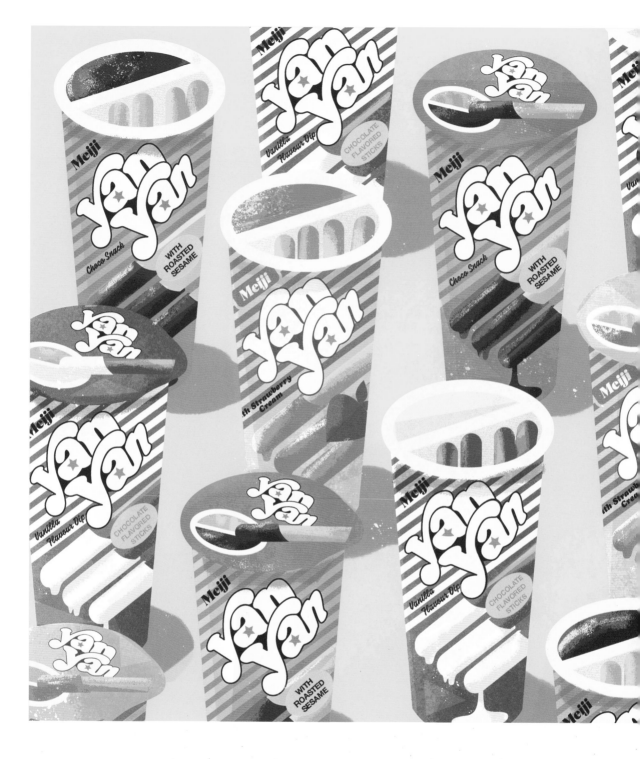

Jake Russell Gavino

[L] Yan Yan Pattern [R] White Rabbit Pattern

[L] Late Night Eats [R] Carne Asada Fries

Jake Russell Gavino

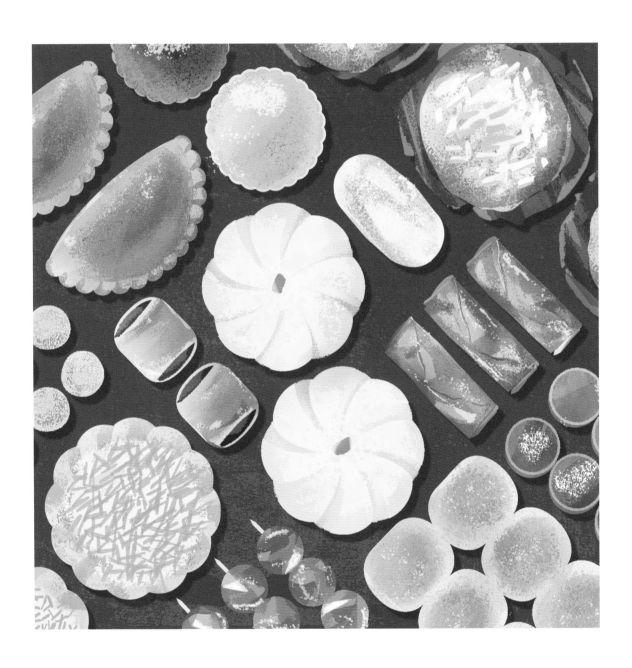

|L| Filipino Feast |R| Filipino Desserts

[L] Taiyaki Pattern [R] Myself as Panda Cookies

Jeannie Phan

[L] Quinoa [R] Coleslaw
Client: Precedent Magazine

I'm not a great cook myself so drawing
is my way of showing food the love it deserves!

Jeannie Phan

[L] Black Bean Dip [R] Yo-Yo Dieting
Client: [L] Precedent Magazine [R] EatingWell Magazine

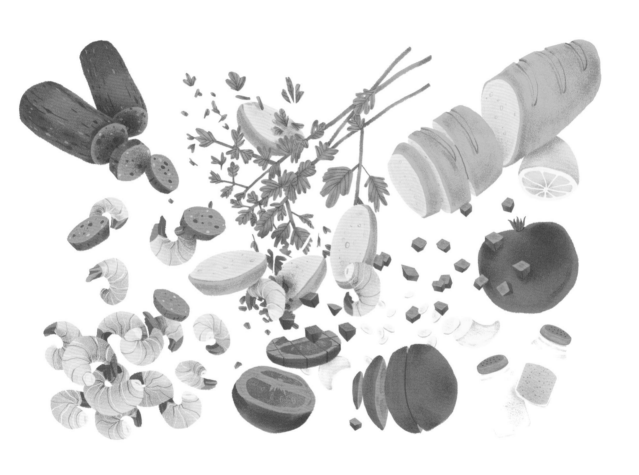

[L] Butter and Scotch [R] Sausage-fest
Client: [L] The New Yorker [R] Precedent Magazine

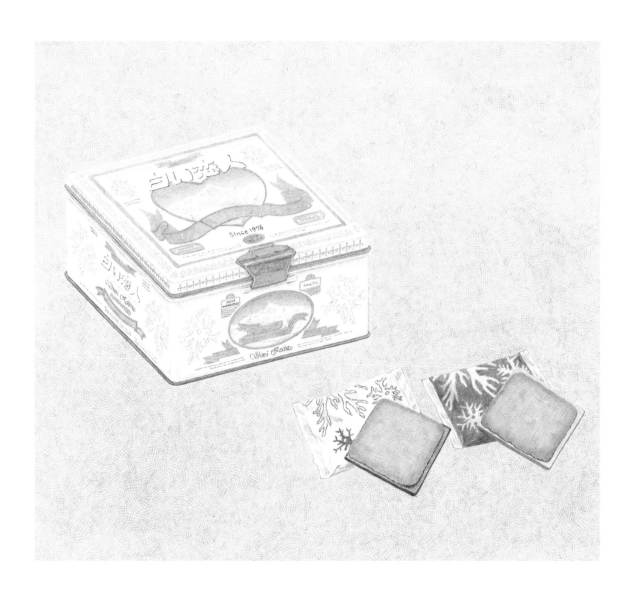

Kaori Doi

[L] Shiroi Koibito (Magazine Cut) [R] Kuzuku Shake (Edo Kuzumochi Brand Concept)
Client: [L] ADUC Inc. [R] Yamashin Shokusan Co., Ltd. | [R] Art Direction: +graphics

Kaori Doi

Illustrations for Retort Pouches 'Gluten-Free' Series
[L] Vegetable Curry / Mushroom and Bean Curry
[R] Minestrone / Corn Soup
Client: Shiseido Parlour Co., Ltd. | Art Direction: VATEAU.

Kaori Doi

[L] Beer Garden [R] Morning Coffee
Client: H'orCafe | Art Direction: Mr. Masaki Hanahara

Kaori Doi

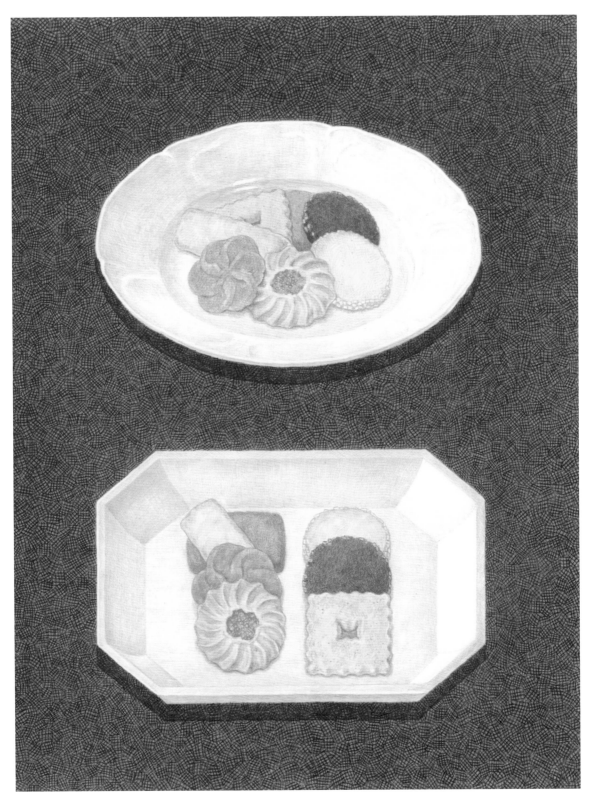

[L][R] Biscuits (Illustrations for 2018AW Catalogue)
Client: Shiseido Parlour Co., Ltd. | Art Direction: VATEAU.

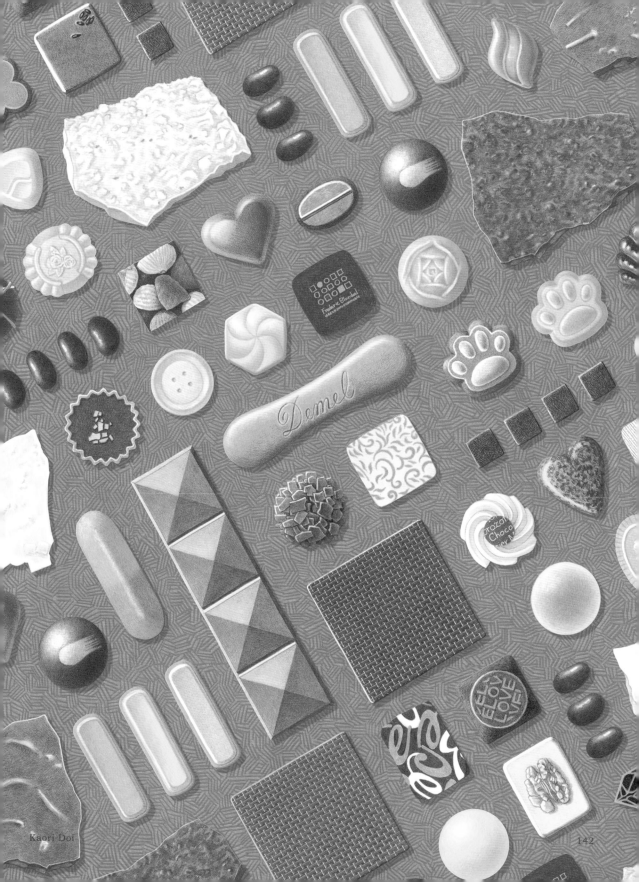

Kaori Doi

142

Chocolates [Main Visual of Valentine's Day Event at Department Stores]
Client: Daimaru Matsuzakaya Department Store Co., Ltd

Parfaits (For Shiseido Parlour Kawasaki Store Signboards)
Client: Shiseido Parlour Co., Ltd.

Alice Chen

[L] Strawberry Custard Tart [R] Cherry Pistachio Tart

[L] Bubble Milk Tea Souffle [R] Croissant Sandwich

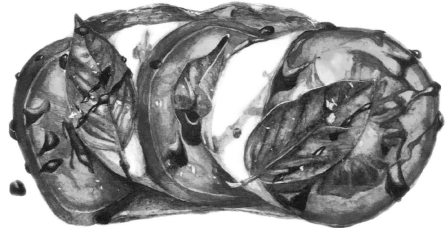

Alice Chen

I like traveling, and delicious food from all over the world. I want to record the best moment of food by my paintings and share them to more people. By doing so, I hope they can not only eat food by their mouths, but also enjoy the beauty of it with their eyes.

MOROHANA CAKE

Morohana Bakery

MOROHANA

Desserts Eaten with Your Eyes:
[L] Vanilla Buttercream Cake [R] Yellow Egg Tart

Desserts Eaten with Your Eyes:
[L] Pink Buttercream Cupcake [R] Lemon Vanilla Cupcake

The fact that I would never see the dessert again once
I eat it, was always one of my bumming points whenever
I eat desserts in a local cafe, it felt like consuming
not only the food itself but the design of it.
So I decided to preserve it on canvas.

MoRoHaNa CaKe

Desserts Eaten with Your Eyes:
[L] Four Assorted Macarons [R] Two-layer Chocolate Cake

MOROHANA CAKE

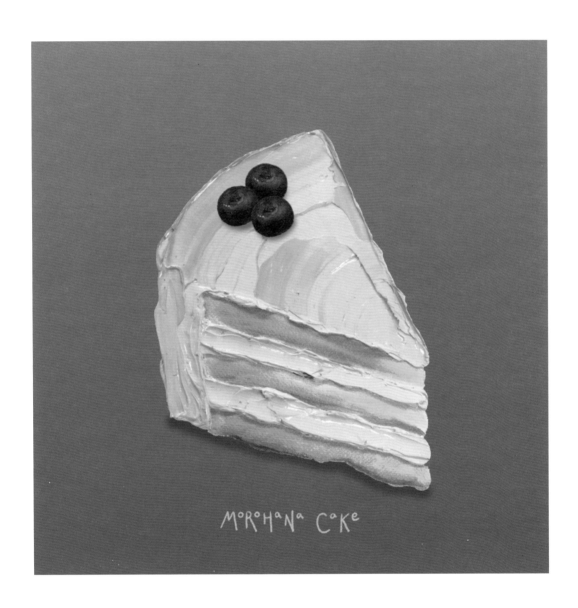

MOROHANA CAKE

Desserts Eaten with Your Eyes:
[L] Lemon Cream Pound Cake [R] Purple Berry Cream Cake Piece

iio / ROOM NUMBER 225

[L||R] yolkasm

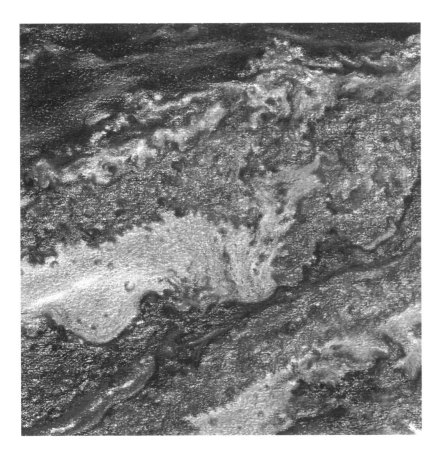

[L][R] yolkasm

Shiho Torii

[L||R] Whipped Cream

Shiho Torii

トリイシホ

[L][R] Whipped Cream

トリイシホ

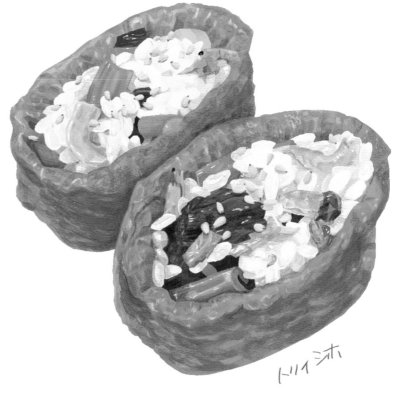

トリイシホ

トリイショホ

[L] Mitarashi Dango / Inari-zushi [R] Monchi Cookies
[Inari-zushi] Client: Morinaga & Co.,LTD.

[L] Buddhist Cuisine [R] Sri Lankan Curry

Linda Liu

[L] Donburi [R] Onigiri / Malay Fish Curry

SO MANY SHAPES!
COLORS! TEXTURES!

[L] Skewers [R] Nabe

Linda Liu

[L] Holiday Spread [R] Xi'an Noodles

Mao Hagiwara

181

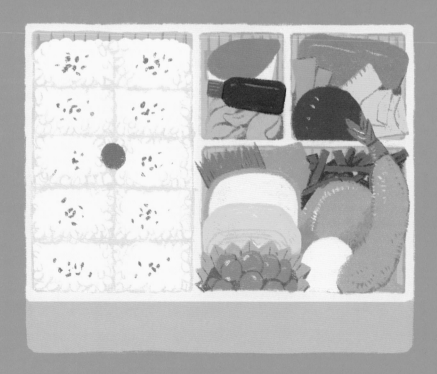

Mao Hagiwara

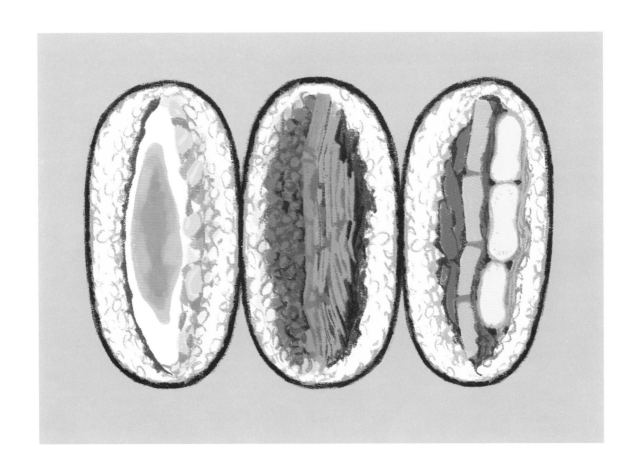

[L||R] Japanese Ramen

Kaitlin Mechan

It is a fun subject matter,
there is so much variety and colour.

Olive oil

garlic

TESCO
OLIVE OIL

TESCO
BOLOGNESE
SAUCE
MADE IN ITALY

Bolognese Sauce

Red onion

Napolina
SPAGHETTI
al dente

Pasta

Quorn
MINCE
300g

cheese

Tomatoes

Quorn mince

Spaghetti bolognese

TESCO
RED SPLIT
LENTILS

HOT
CURRY
powder

MUSTARD
SEEDS

Diana Dagadita

[L] Still Here Still Life: Sushi Party [R] Veggie Cat
[L] Special Credit: Cecilia Rose McCormick

[L] Pantry: Groceries [R] Rainbow Chard
[R] Client: Ian Brice

I think I like to draw food because it's universally loved and relatable. Rich in textures, colours and shapes, food is always a subject I enjoy experimenting with.

Especially when trying out a new drawing technique, I tend to turn to food for a safe and familiar subject that lends itself to transformation — much like cooking, the ingredients are often the same, but there are so many combinations and ways to reinvent them!

Cooking is a human experience, an ocasion for culture sharing for kindness, for pleasure.

Drawing food is just more accessible...

[L] Pantry: Coconut Milk / Hazelnut Milk / Raspberry Jam / Pesto and Sundried Tomatoes

Anke Knapper

[L] Breakfast [R] Tea and Toast
[R] Client: Visie

Vegetarian Food
Client: De Volkskrant

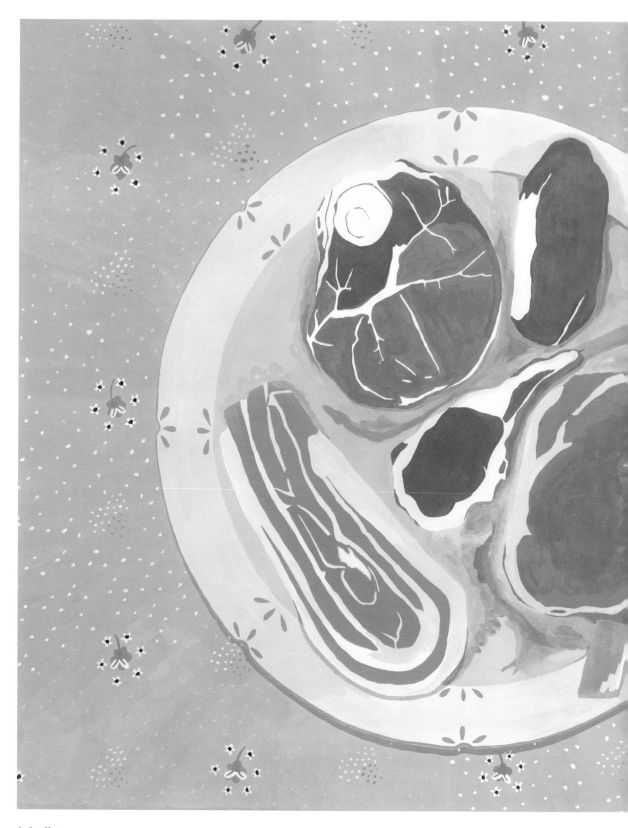

Anke Knapper

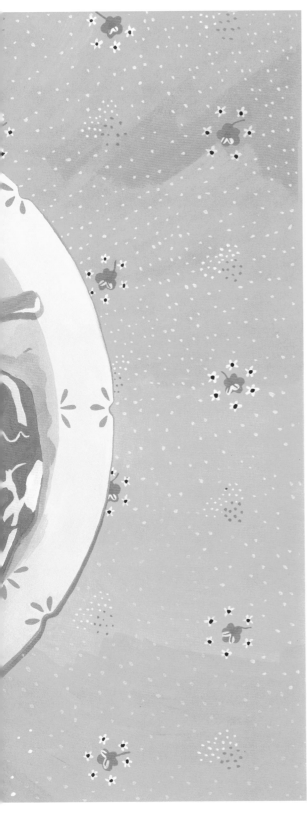

Anke Knapper

[L] Kitchen [R] Lemonade
[R] Client: Visie

Because I love to eat it!
(who doesn't?)

[L] Vegetarian BBQ
Client: Elle Eten

Yasuko Hayakawa

Let's Eat: [L] Tea Time [R] Delicious Cheese

Let's Eat: ⌊L⌋ Strawberry Tart / Margherita ⌊R⌋ Udon / Fruit Cake

Yasuko Hayakawa

Let's Eat: [L] Japanese Confectionery [R] Berliner Pfannkuchen

Fraisier
フレジエ

表面に ピンクの マジパンを 乗せた
フランスの いちごケーキ。

Gâteau Basque
ガト・バスク

Let's Eat: [L] Fraisier [R] Gateau Basque

Yasuko Hayakawa

Let's Eat: [L] Japanese Confectionery 2 [R] Japanese Food

Shuku Nishi

shuku.

I think food and eating is very important.
It's filled with more important things
than nutrition and filling the stomach.

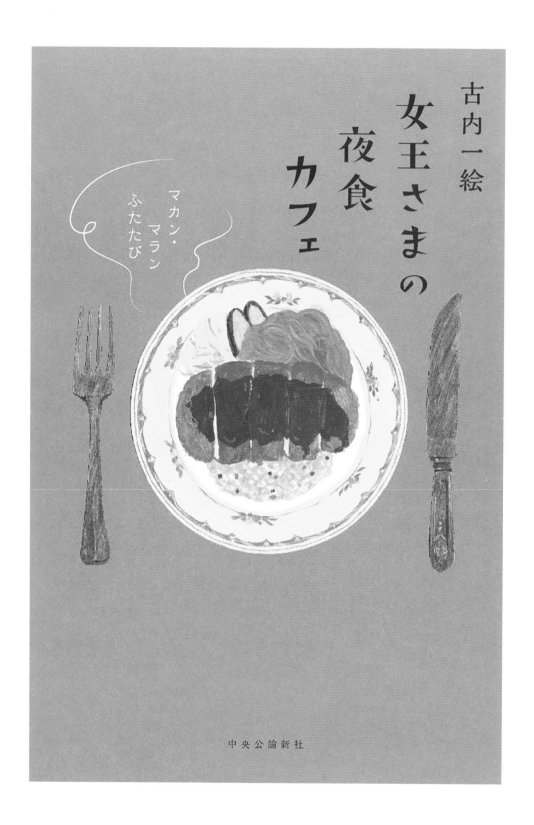

古内一絵

女王さまの
夜食
カフェ

マカン・
マラン
ふたたび

中央公論新社

[L][R] 'Makan Malam' Book Cover
Client/Special Credit: Misato Yamamoto (Chuoukouron Shinsha)

It is considered unlucky to ha

Alice Pattullo

guests at the dinner table.

BREAD BAKED MUST BE EATEN.

Village Voice Choice Eats
Client: Village Voice Choice Eats Annual Tasting Event

Yon Park

Croissant
with Coffee
in the morning

Yon Park

When I was young, I went to a family restaurant named "COCOS".
The caramel pudding decorated with a cute flag fluttered me.
It's little bit weird that I still remember how I felt.

When I first saw the pudding, though I cannot figure out how delicious it was.
This kind of experience let me know sometimes the visual image
of the food can make people happier than the taste itself.

I can say if a chef can make food delicious,
I can make food more adorable. Not only the decoration of the food,
but also the comfort image of the food can also touch someone's mind.
I believe I can make some people feel happy with my food paintings.

[L] Cheese Fondue

PICKLES

Jalapeño

Vegetable Pickle

Carrot

CABBAGE

Asparagus pickle

ASPARAGUS FRESH VEGETABLE AND VINEGAR

mixed vegetable pickle

CUCUMBER

ONION

VEGETABLE

Pistachio

Macadamia

peanut

Acorn

pine nut

nut

Walnut

Almond

HAZEL NUT

Pecan & pecan pie

Cacao and nibs

Cashew nut

Zena Kay

[L] Roasted Mackerel [R] Lobster Platter
[L] Client / Special Credit: Dishes to Delight, Bre Graham

Zena Kay

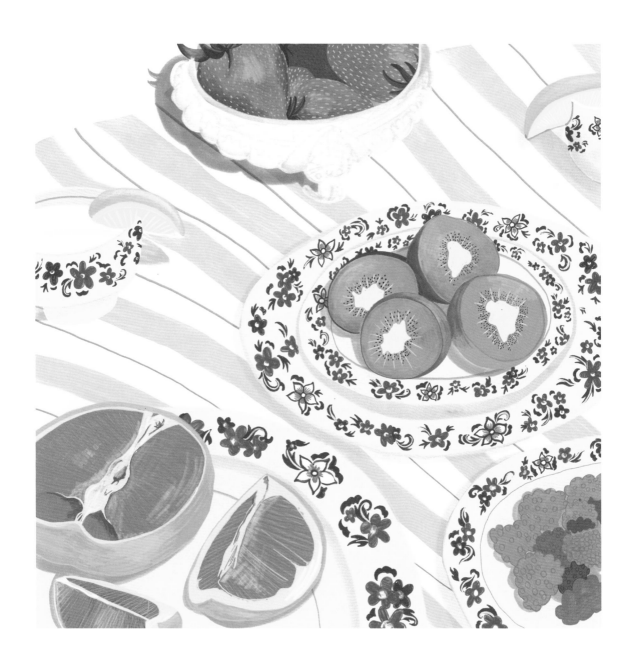

[L] Watermelon & Radish [R] Fruity Selection
Client: Still Here Still Life | Special Credit: [L] Laura Schoorl [R] Rebecca Alaniz

Why the hell not draw food!
Its bloody delicous. Originally
I wanted to study baking or
cooking but decided strangely
to go to Art School + keep cooking as
a hobby! (chefs scared me haha!) Always keeping
food in mind and collecting
endless amounts of cookbooks with
my student loan, I would draw
Recipes etc which I cooked. I soon
realised that food illustration was
a thing!

For me I love how food
brings people together, very much
inspired by the spanish term Sombremessa!
The best feeling is that point in the meal
where no one speaks and everyone just's
experiences the flavours which feels alot like
when you go to a gallery and you observe and
appreciate the painting. taking in every last
brush stock! Thats why and why I love
drawing, painting food. The feeling of people
coming together and connecting!

Enid Din

Drawing & looking at food art brings back memories -
most of which are warm, happy and times filled with love.
I want to often relive and share these moments
so I draw them a lot. Aside from that,
textures & colors found in food interests me a lot.

Enid Din

248

Hanming Wang

[L] Summer Picnic [R] Déjeuner au Soleil - Lunch in the Sun
Special Credit (Photo Reference): [L] Bloom & Wild [R] Casa Viola

Hanming Wang

Food brings people together.

Strawberries

gooseberries
redcurrants

hazelnuts

🇩🇰 DANISH LAGKAGE

gooseberry
& elderflower
jam

[L] Sunday Brunch in the Garden. Alfresco Dining Made Perfect [R] Danish Lagkage (Layered Cake)
Special Credit (Photo Reference): [L] Kirthanaa Naidu [R] Plate Talks

Hanming Wang

Labels within illustration: BLUE POOL, Fanny's, SUN SEAKER

[L] Yellow Tulips and Cheese [R] Oysters for Dinner Tonight
Special Credit (Photo Reference): [L] Laura Schoorl [R] Humpback Singapore

Hanming Wang

[L] If Life Gives You Apples, Make An Apple Pie [R] Ice Cream Cake
[R] Special Credit (Photo Reference): Bre Graham

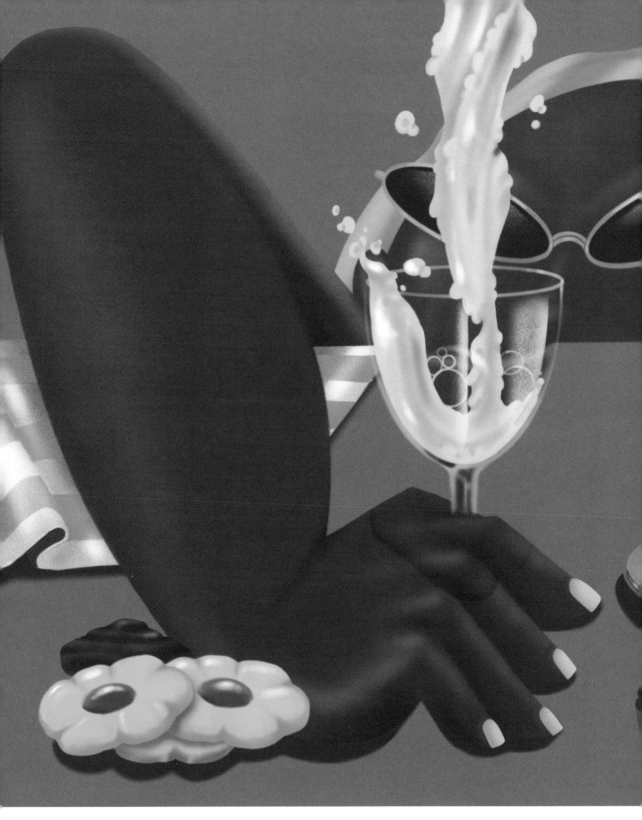

Patricia Doria

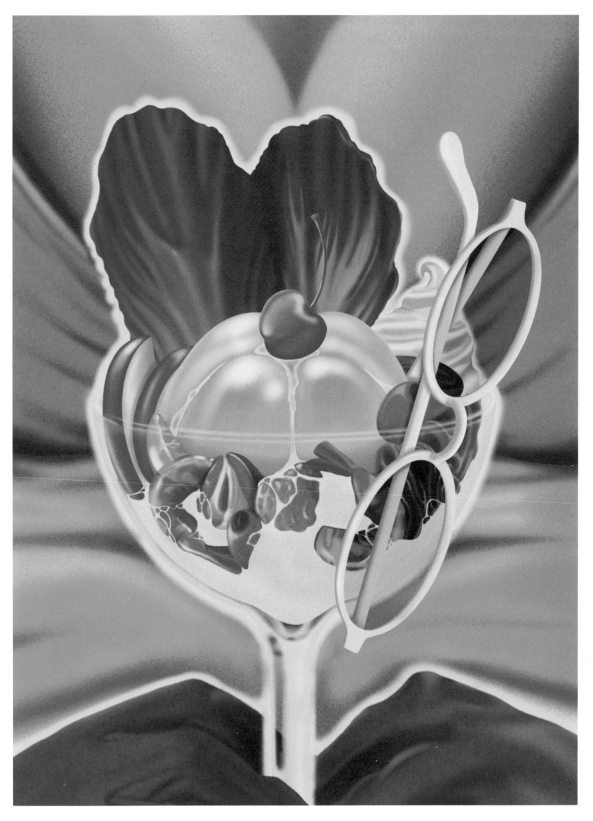

Patricia Doria

As a child, I have always loved scanning
through food magazines. I guess that
carried on as an adult.

Food as a subject matter in an
artwork is like cheating.
Because food is art in itself.

[L] Savory Sweet Delight [R] Hello Apple

Jialei Sun

[L][R] Bread

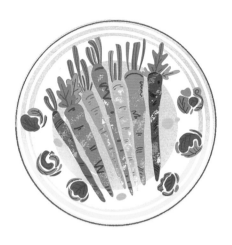

The only reason of drawing food is because I'm fond of eating them. I love searching around for delicious food, and watching videos about food. In the days of quarantine we have no chance to go outside, it's also very hard to get up early and have a good breakfast. I usually have bread for breakfast when living in the US, after have had white bread for 3 weeks, I really think it's time to make some changes. Some people told me that I can make bread by my own, but... I'm not very interested in it. So I made the series of bread illustrations to pretend I 'had' a great breakfast everyday. By the way, I'm still having white bread for breakfast.

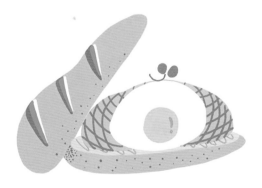

Lucia Pham

fish sauce

cloud ear fungus

mushroom

pickle

vegetables

onion

olive oil

kohlrabi

beef

pea

mushroom

paprika

lettuce

apple cider avinegar

chili pepper

herb

egg-beater

fish sauce

cucumber

carrot

cherry tomato

garlic

egg

shrimp

lime

FRESH SPRING ROLL

herb

Vietnamese Cuisine

Q WHY DO YOU LIKE / CHOOSE TO DRAW (ABOUT) FOOD ?

A I am a soulful person with food. Eating is my greatest pleasure, then drawing ☺. I have a habit of capturing the delicious food I've tasted, and I will draw them into posters with captions & cute expressions as a personal project to improve my drawing skills.
Drawing food also makes me feel better, because is there anyone who doesn't like food ?

Q WHAT IS THE yummiest THING you've TASTED IN YOUR LIFE (AND WHY / WHERE) ?

A Vietnamese Food ! FRIED SPRING ROLL !!

Rice NOODLE

DIPPING SAUCE

< NEM RA'N >
FRIED SPRING ROLL

I think spring roll is the quintessence of Vietnamese cuisine ! No Vietnamese do not love fried spring rolls. Spring rolls is love spring rolls is life ! This is a dish that you can taste meat (pork), herbs, spices in a bite ! And the best fried spring rolls I ever ate belonged to my mom ! My mom makes spring rolls everytime family members crave it and it's awesome ALL THE TIME !!! ♥ ♥

What is the yummiest thing you've ever tasted in your life?

My most memorable dessert. It's from a French dessert shop in Taipei. Called Agnès b. Café. That's a French dessert shop I accidentally discovered. The glass cabinet is filled with many very exquisite and delicious French pastries, like jewelry.

I was attracted to the past.

I ordered a chestnut chocolate Montblanc. I was very surprised. The cross-section of the cake is a combination of several layers, so delicate that there is a thin layer of chocolate in the middle of the cake and the cake, which makes the cake more changes in taste. A small cake can match so many flavors and textures. It was the best dessert I had ever tasted and I had never tasted it. This completely subverted my mind.

Alice Chen

Family Meal

Boiled pasta in the leftover soup of acqua pazza with mussels. It's a taste from my memories of 'Les Hydropathes', a Belgian beer bar in Tokyo which has closed down, so it's something you can never taste again.

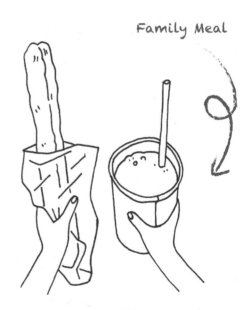

Ayu Iwashima

YOUTIAO AND FRESH SOY MILK IN TAIWAN. I STILL DREAM ABOUT THE SPONGY BUT CRISP BITE OF THE YOUTIAO AFTER DUNKING IT IN THE SWEET MILK. I WISH I COULD HAVE THIS FOR BREAKFAST EVERYDAY!

Grated apples, which I ate when I had a cold as a child, were always the most delicious.

Grated apple

Bento

And the Bento that my mother used to make every day when I was in high school.

Most recently, I had a delicious sandwich lunch made by my nine-year-old son.

Sandwich lunch

Hatsue Fujiyasu

Shiho Torii

Because I like eating and every time I eat something delicious, it makes me want drawing. It's so fun !!!

Last summer I went to California with my friends, I've had one of the most delicious Benedict I've ever had over there. So pity that I can't remember the name of that cafe..,
"Republique" or something?

Jialei Sun

Beef stew. Fluffy egg on rice cooked by a Japanese uncle in Hakone.
There are only 8 seats in the tiny restaurant, and only two items on the menu.
The chef takes his time to cook every single dish in the exact Methodical way.
I will never forget it.

Hanming Wang

And I love to draw transparent and colorful things!

Tablet flavoured ice cream on the Isle of Arran.

Kaitlin Mechan

In 2011, I had breakfast with a Turkish family.
It was simple but varied: two kind of pickled
olives, freshly cut tomatoes, Mozzarella cheese,
peanut balls, two or three kinds of bread
(salty round bread, bread toast, hard raisin bread crust.),
coffe, peants, boiled eggs, ham,
and countless plates and flatware....

It seemed that watherver was available at home
was served, and the whole table was full of food.

It was a breakfast I had with my firend's family
in Turkey. The food was common home-cooked food.
but the sunshine. well arranged environment,
and nice people that morning made the meal
exceptional, and I couldn't forget it
after all these years.

Claire Chien

YAGEN NANKOTSU

薬研軟骨

A type of yakitori, a traditional
Japanese dish of grilled chicken cartilage.
From the first time I ate it until now,
it has always been the most delicious
and I love it!

Yuko Kurihara

It's "UNI" of Hokkaido.
Because it is fresh.
It melts in the mouth.

Midori Asano

Over the summer I went on a trip to Suffolk (UK)
with my family. We had lunch one day at 'L'Escargot Sur-Mer'
— One of London's oldest restaurant's, which had opened a pop-up
in Suffolk in an attempt to save its entire workforce (the
Soho restaurant was closed due to Covid19.) I had half a
lobster cooked in garlic butter — it was my first time eating
lobster, and it was the *most delicious* thing I've ever eaten!

Jordan Amy Lee

Xuetong Wang

strawberries sold in supermarket
↳ A lot bigger than wildstrawbery

I bought them from an old lady In China.

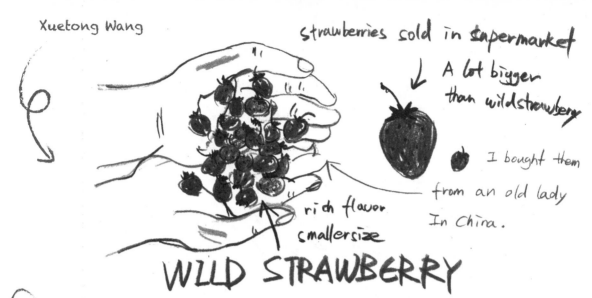

rich flavor
smaller size

WLLD STRAWBERRY

Shuku Nishi

A salted rice ball made by my mother.
I think it's the most delicious food in the world for me.

I can't think of a single thing, because as long as the food is not extremely terrible, it is fine by me!

DONMAK & CO.

It's "Kiyomi" Ramen in Shizuoka prefecture in Japan. We can eat it in SoBA restrant neaby Shizuoka Station.
It's so yummy because it has good soup made Soy sauce, "tonkotsu" and "Dashi"!

Mao Hagiwara

I love all my mother's cooking that has full of details such as broth, ingredients, time, effort, and arrangement.

Kaori Doi

Lucia Calfapietra

I ADORE ramen, but I only tasted it in Paris because I've never been to Japan!

The yummiest thing hmm... hard to choose, but the first thing that comes to mind must be Tom Yum soup. It was back in December 2019 around Christmas - my work colleagues and I had a pajama party where we had to bring homemade food to share, and as we come from four different countries, it was a real joy of discovery.

The Tom Yum soup was so unexpected, I'd never had anything like it before! I ended up having seconds. I loved it so, so much and still think fondly of it and the loveliest people who made it. ♡

Diana Dagadita

This pie baked by my friend Caroline, she brought it with her when she came to visit our newborn son, Julius ♡.

We finished the whole pie in one day.

Anke Knapper

It's a very difficult question. Home-made 'Gukbab' is the best these days. (Gukbab – Korean beef and rice soup) Eating something warm makes my heart warm.

Xiha

286

The most unforgettable taste in my life
is the 'Rainbow fresh cream cake'
from West Gin Bakery in South Korea.

I greatly enjoy tasting the 7 differently colored
whipped cream. There is no difference in taste
by the color but I eat in a whole-cake size
every month whenever I feel stressful.

It is like eating and seeing a rainbow
every month.

Morohana Bakery

I can't forget the taste of the fig
grown in my grandmother's garden.
I/e always likes figs.

Keiji Yano

My mom's pancit palabok
is the tastiest thing I've ever
eaten. my mom cooks it for me
whenever I come to visit.

Jake Russell Gavino

Freshly caught

grilled Mahi-Mahi
SIARGAO ISLAND, PHILIPPINES

Patricia Doria

Knowing the history of the food I'm eating now sometimes makes me thrilled.
A few days ago, I visited my friend's house located in the middle of mountain,
located in the middle of Seoul. Her house is quite disparate in that this place
keep calm, inspirational and unique atmosphere in the center of one of the busiest city
in the world. She introduce me her kitchen garden and treated me lunch,
consists of organic salad just harvested in the garden and whole wheat bread.

While having lunch, she explained the history of the food like how many times
she watered them and so on. I can feel her soft touch to the food in every single bite.
The atmosphere around us was warm, and the wind was tender. It couldn't be better.

Yon Park

The yummiest thing I have eaten. Thats a really hard question. I often associate this with the experience and who I am with but theres probably two meals which just bring me so much comfort! One being a dhal!!! Curry or anything Indian in general! I remember going to india and experiencing my first 5p Samosa cooked by a lovely older lady who was just so happy for me to be trying her food! I also often think about a home cooked dhal and pickled paneer dish my brother makes. We probably eat this once a week + love cooking it for others, hence why we started the supper club 'shared plates', ran by mysely, brother and Sophie (brothers partener) its a real family affair.

Another fond memory of food eaten is back when I lived in portugal, despite this memory including an awful ex, the food overlooks this. Its back when me and friends went to the fishing village and we ate endless amounts of bbq'd sardines, octopus, shrimps and cod fish served with buttery potatoes and fresh garlicy vegetables! + of course lots of wine + portuguese port! I still dream of the day I can live in portugal again!

I think the yummiest foods I've eaten are always in the Countries they come from! This is why Mexico is my hopefully next destination!

Zena Kay

One of the most delicious things I've ever eaten was an 'Oyako-don' from a restaurant called 'Ohana', in Kawagoe, Japan.

Victoria Moey

PORK RIND JELLY

Linda Liu

Robatayaki of salmon that we ate in Sapporo. Hokkaido, Japan a year ago.

Harapekomegane

288

It's '된장찌개', Doenjang - jjigae or Korean soybean paste stew in English, which is one of the most common and representative '찌개' recipes in Korean home meals. A mouthful of hot bean curd, zucchini and 된장 soup is drawn in my head, whenever I need warmth deep in my body.

Not special, not fancy, but I'm always glad to smell 된장찌개 with the sound my mom chops and boils something for the dinner.

iio / ROOM NUMBER 225

Mom's homemade pho!
It's understated but home-y and nostalgic.
It's all I need in a meal.

Jeannie Phan

Enid Din

Tita Betty's Sinigang
(My aunts' sinigang).
Can't help eating lots of it!!!

Too hard to recall or choose just one thing...
However, I get quite nostalgic for certain meals -
I still think my mum's cheese and potato pie might
be my favourite meal!

Alice Pattullo

"Shirayaki" of ell that I ate in Mishima
Shizuoka Prefecture.

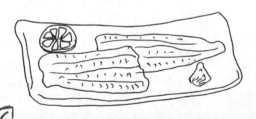

Hiroyuki Yamada

It's the rice porridge
that my mother used to
make for me when I was a child
and had a cold.

The food was
hot and salty.
and made me
feel better.

Yasuko Hayakawa

Alice Chen
@illustration_in_wonderland

Alice Chen is a painter and illustrator with a strong passion for art. Based in Taiwan, she loves travelling and is inspired by delicious flavours from all around the world.

PP. 146-151, 282

Ayu Iwashima
ayuiwashima.com

Ayu Iwashima is an illustrator who was born—and continues to live—in Tokyo. She enjoys cooking and spending time in nature, making them the main themes of her illustrations.

PP. 050-055, 282

Alice Pattullo
alicepattullo.com

Alice Pattullo is an illustrator based in East London who regularly explores British traditions, folklore, and superstitions in her personal work, producing limited edition screen prints for sale. She also works on commissioned illustrations for a variety of clients, often with a focus on food-based illustration.

PP. 226-231, 289

Claire Chien
@claire.chien1

Claire Chien was a graphic designer in a design company for close to 10 years before making the switch to freelancing in 2015. She currently runs her own illustration business.

PP. 084-091, 284

Anke Knapper
ankeknapper.com

Anke Knapper is a freelance illustrator who draws stories about everyday subjects and experiences, as well as her favourite things like food, mysteries, science, history, nature, taboos, and travelling. Born in Assen, she now lives and works in The Hague.

PP. 200-209, 286

Claire Harrup
claireharrup.com

Claire Harrup is an illustrator and printmaker living in the UK, whose work utilises both traditional and digital means of production. Her commercial illustrations have been used on packaging, books, and products around the world.

PP. 026-033

Diana Dagadita

ephemre.com

Diana Dagadita is a Romanian freelance illustrator and printmaker currently based in London. Her personal work revolves around the fleeting aspects of life, encompassing memories, feelings, nostalgia, nature, light-and-shadows, food, domestic comforts, and the beauty of the mundane.

PP. 194-199, 286

Family Meal

@familymeal.shop

Based in sunny Manila with a background in running restaurants, Family Meal makes art and merchandise for people who love food.

PP. 112-119, 282

DONMAK & CO.

donmak.hk

Born and raised in Hong Kong, Don Mak is an illustrator who co-founded his eponymous studio in 2016. His passion and artistry stem from the time he spent with local comic artists in his early working years, during which he honed his vivid storytelling style.

PP. 098-105, 285

Hanming Wang

hanmingcollection.com

For Hanming, an artist in Singapore, art is a way to slow down, connect with her inner self, and pay attention to analogue details in the 'now'. She captures small yet meaningful moments as a ritual to appreciate and celebrate life.

PP. 252-259, 283

Enid Din

be.net/eniddin

Enid Din is an illustrator from Manila with a penchant for drawing plants, food, and slices of life.

PP. 246-251, 289

Harapekomegane

harapekomegane.com

Husband-and-wife duo Shinya Harada and Kaori Seki work together as an illustration unit based in Japan.

PP. 106-111, 288

Hatsue Fujiyasu

fujiyasu.wixsite.com/illustration

Born in Fukushima and currently based
in Tokyo, Hatsue Fujiyasu was schooled
in art and design from the University of
Tsukuba. Fujiyasu's dignified and beautiful
illustrations often feature landscapes with
houses and towers, food, old knick-knacks,
and people.

PP. 034-039, 283

Jake Russell Gavino

jakegavino.com

Jake Gavino is a Bay Area-based graphic
designer with a penchant for illustration.
Currently designing for globally-renowned
clients at Turner Duckworth, he enjoys
work that is both strategic and conceptual,
while also being playful and fun.

PP. 120-127, 287

Hiroyuki Yamada

tis-home.com/hiroyuki-yamada

Illustrator Hiroyuki Yamada was born in
Kyoto in 1961 and graduated from the Kyoto
Saga Art Junior College in 1982. Winner of
Japan's Good Design Award for S&B Spice
& Herb's packaging illustration in 2006, his
works have been selected for various poster
competitions all around the world.

PP. 008-017, 289

Jeannie Phan

jeanniephan.com

Jeannie Phan is an internationally published
Vietnamese-Canadian illustrator whose work
often appears in editorials, books, and brands.
Born in Winnipeg, she eventually relocated
to Toronto, where she is currently based and
actively practicing illustration, to attend OCAD
University before graduating with honours.

PP. 128-133, 289

iio | ROOM NUMBER 225

roomnumber225.com

iio is a portraitist and publisher
based in Korea.

PP. 160-165, 289

Jialei Sun

jialeisun.website

Jialei Sun is a bird lover and freelance
illustrator based in Baltimore. She enjoys
making cute art pieces and adding her
own humorous twists to them.

PP. 264-271, 283

Jordan Amy Lee
jordanamylee.com

Jordan Amy Lee is a London-based illustrator who draws inspiration from the shapes and forms found in everyday life. She uses stripped-back compositions, bold colours, and delicate textures to turn a simple object into an eye-catching illustration.

PP. 062-067, 284

Keiji Yano
yano-keiji.com

Born in Japan's Kochi prefecture, Keiji Yano graduated with a Master's degree from the Tokyo University of the Arts in 2011 before working at Nintendo as a 3D designer. He became an illustrator at OFFICE YANO in 2017.

PP. 040-043, 287

Kaitlin Mechan
kaitlinmechan.myportfolio.com

Kaitlin Mechan is a freelance illustrator based in Scotland.

PP. 188-193, 283

Linda Liu
lindersliu.com

Linda Liu is a hungry illustrator with a taste for tactile textures, saucy shapes, and palatable palettes. She graduated from Rhode Island School of Design and is currently working as a designer and freelance illustrator. She enjoys making meals on paper and eating meals in reality.

PP. 174-179, 288

Kaori Doi
doikaori.com

Kaori Doi was majoring in pottery at Musashino Art University before dropping out to pursue a career in web design and direction. She has always painted as a hobby—even as a child—but only started drawing in earnest after getting married.

PP. 134-145, 285

Lucia Calfapietra
luciacalfapietra.com

Lucia Calfapietra is an Italian illustrator based in France, whose work can be found on magazines, books, and packaging. She plays with textures, clean shapes, and vivid colours with a retro vibe – food being one of her favourites topics. She often collaborates with graphic designer and lettering artist Nicolò Giacomin.

PP. 056-061, 285

Lucia Pham
luciapham.com

Lucia Pham is an independent visual artist from Vietnam who specialises in illustration, graphic design, and art direction. She loves using bright, eye-catching colours and different shapes to illustrate people and life.

PP. 272-280

Mao Hagiwara
maohagiwara.com

Mao Hagiwara is an illustrator based in Shizuoka, Japan.

PP. 180-187, 285

Midori Asano
komidori.jugem.jp

Born in Tokyo, Midori Asano is an illustrator based in Saitama who graduated from the Joshibi Junior College of Art and Design.

PP. 044-049, 284

Morohana Bakery
@morohana_bakery

Morohana Bakery is a food illustrator and oil painter who bakes desserts on paper, not in an oven.

PP. 152-159, 287

Patricia Doria
@petdoria

Patricia Doria is an illustrator in Manila who currently works as an in-house creative at a retail company. She enjoys drawing even in her spare time.

PP. 260-263, 287

Shiho Torii
toriishiho.net

Shiho Torii is a Shizuoka-based illustrator and manga creator who draws for corporate advertisements, picture books, magazines, and teaching materials.

PP. 166-173, 283

Shuku Nishi
nishishuku.net

Shuku Nishi is an illustrator and painter in Japan whose art has been featured in books, advertisements, and TV commercials, as well as on CD covers and packaging. Taking inspiration from nature, she also creates block prints, oil paintings, and three-dimensional works.

PP. 220-225, 285

Victoria Moey
@plate.to.paper

Victoria Moey is a food illustrator and multidisciplinary artist from Singapore working under the name Plate.to.Paper. She believes that food, in its creation and design, is a powerful method of expression and something that brings people from all walks of life together.

Xiha
@xiha_nation

Xiha, the work name of Im So Yeon, is an illustrator from Korea.

Xuetong Wang
tongw.me

...ng graduated from the Maryland College of
...an MFA in illustration. Currently based
...k, she uses illustration as a means of
...on, visually and conceptually. Her
...lined by beauty and accuracy.

...akawa
...om

...illustrator
...scapes,

Yon Park
@artist.yonpark

A major in fine art and textile design, Yon Park expresses herself by exploring delicious food and healthy ingredients wherever she goes. Inspired by small yet fanciful things and atypically-crafted objects, she is an illustrator obsessed with the petit part of nature.

Yuko Kurihara
yuko-kurihara.com

Yuko Kurihara's unique style is rooted in traditional Japanese painting techniques. The Tokyo-based artist and illustrator expresses the beauty of vegetables by highlighting nature's colours, shapes and patterns like the holes on leaves left by insects and the unruliness of growing roots, celebrating their microscopic details.

Zena Kay
zenaokay.com

Zena is an illustrator and foodie based in Nottingham. Passionate about celebrating the beauty of food, still life, nature, travel, and interiors, she weaves stories through shapes and colours.

Acknowledgements

We would like to thank all the designers, studios, and companies who were involved in the production of this book for their significant contribution to its compilation. We would also like to express our gratitude to all the producers involved for their invaluable opinions and assistance, as well as the professionals in the creative industry who were generous with their insights and feedback throughout the entire production process. Last but not least, to those who made specific input behind the scenes but were not credited in this book, we acknowledge and appreciate all your effort and continuous support.

Future Editions

If you wish to participate in viction:ary's future projects and publications, please send your website or portfolio to: submit@victionary.com